A CONCISE HISTORY OF

AFRICA

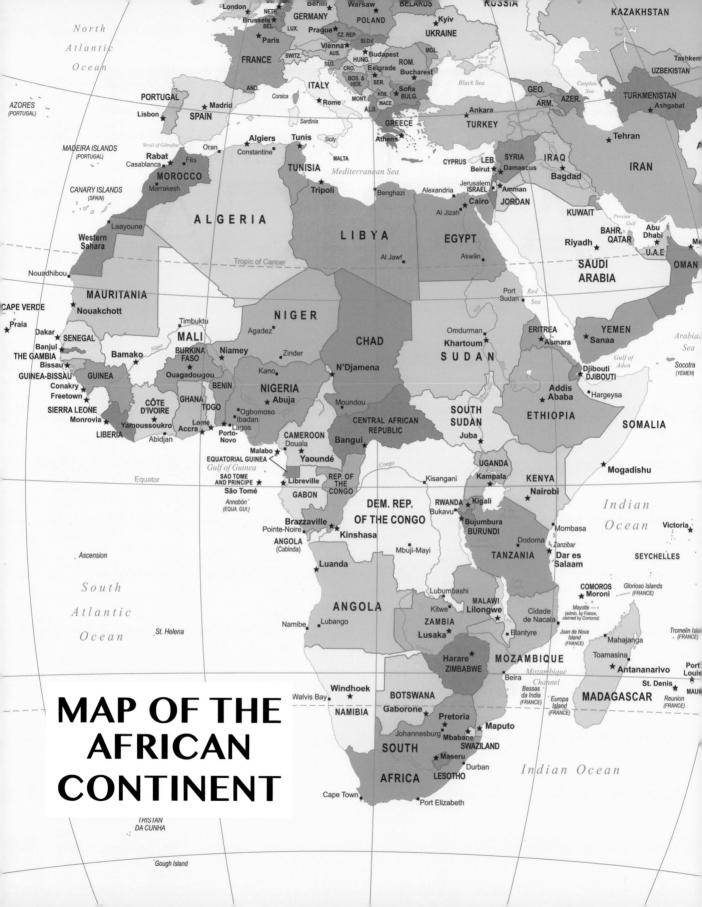

MAP OF THE AFRICAN CONTINENT

A CONCISE HISTORY OF
AFRICA

Annelise Hobbs

MASON CREST

Mason Crest
450 Parkway Drive, Suite D
Broomall, PA 19008
www.masoncrest.com

Cataloging-in-Publication Data on file with the Library of Congress

Printed and bound in the United States of America.

First printing
9 8 7 6 5 4 3 2 1

ISBN: 978-1-4222-3716-8
Series ISBN: 978-1-4222-3715-1
ebook ISBN: 978-1-4222-8067-6
ebook series ISBN: 978-1-4222-8066-9

Produced by Regency House Publishing Limited
The Manor House
High Street
Buntingford
Hertfordshire
SG9 9AB
United Kingdom

www.regencyhousepublishing.com

Text copyright © 2017 Regency House Publishing Limited/Annelise Hobbs

CONTENTS

KEY ICONS TO LOOK FOR:

Words to Understand: These words with their easy-to-understand definitions will increase the reader's understanding of the text, while building vocabulary skills.

Sidebars: This boxed material within the main text allows readers to build knowledge, gain insights, explore possibilities, and broaden their perspectives by weaving together additional information to provide realistic and holistic perspectives.

Text-Dependent Questions: These questions send the reader back to the text for more careful attention to the evidence presented there.

A herd of wild elephants (*Loxodonta africana*) in the Serengeti National Park which is an UNESCO World Heritage Site in Tanzania.

AFRICA: WHO DREW THE LINES?

During the late 1870s and early 1880s King Leopold II of Belgium had been furthering his interests by laying claim to land along the lower Congo river, an area to which Portugal had already staked a claim. In 1884 Germany's first chancellor, Otto von Bismarck, announced German claims to three African colonies: Togoland, Cameroon, and South-West Africa, which threatened to create a state of conflict, there being concerns over the European colonial balance of power. Bismarck, with France, called for a conference to settle these rivalries, and it was on November

LEFT: King Leopold II of Belgium lay claim to lands along the lower Congo river.

BELOW LEFT: Germany's first Chancellor Otto von Bismarck.

BELOW: A Masai tribesman herding goats.

15, 1884 that the Berlin West Africa Conference began. Formally dressed, diplomats from 14 European nations and the United States of America came to the table, the purpose of the meeting ostensibly being humanitarian concerns for Africa.

Hitherto, the Europeans had confined themselves to coastal Africa, and had avoided venturing inland for fear of yellow fever, malaria, and the nameless hazards associated with the "Dark Continent." Now, the "Scramble for Africa," that had begun slowly in the 1870s, would be accelerated, and the race to obtain "spheres of influence" within the continent's interior would be continued in earnest. This would reach its peak towards the end of the 19th century, and only begin to diminish during the first decade of the next.

Many believe the European nations divided African land between themselves as they sat at the table in Berlin, but in fact this had already been happening for some years. The Berlin Conference only served to recognize the status quo and was largely meaningless, yet it emphasized Europe's unquestioned attitude of superiority, indicating they were poised to take over the continent, which they would accomplish over the next 25 years; lines would be cut across traditional borders, ignoring ethnic, linguistic, and cultural groups to create nations of disparate people who would not necessarily have much in common.

Beginning in the 1950s, the colonies regained their independence over the next 40 years, but the rapidity of the process was to bring unrest and instability that continues to this day.

CRADLE OF MANKIND?

There are several countries claiming to be the "Cradle of Civilization": the Tigris-Euphrates region in modern-day Syria and Iraq; the Indus Valley in the Indian subcontinent; the Huang He-Yangtze river basins in China; and the Nile valley, with Africa having the remains, in Egypt, of the great Pharaonic civilization. But the origins of mankind are altogether more difficult to pinpoint.

Genetic evidence seems to support the single-origin theory, so it was all the more exciting when, in 2007, researchers at Cambridge University, England, announced that, after analyzing thousands of skulls from around the world, they had reached the conclusion that humankind originated in a single

Words to Understand

Civilization: The stage of human social development and organization that is considered most advanced.

Islam: The religion of the Muslims, a faith regarded as revealed through Muhammad as the Prophet of Allah.

Precolonial: Relating to a period of time before colonization of a region or territory.

area of sub-Saharan Africa some 50,000 years ago.

This would seem to echo a dramatic "new" theory that caused a furore in the late 1980s, that modern man derived from a single African female, although claims of

her being the "mother of mankind" were then called into doubt. What is not in doubt is the work, begun in the early 1930s and continuing to this day, of three generations of the Leakey family, whose first breakthrough was to discover the remains of early hominid types at the Olduvai Gorge and Laetoli in the Great Rift Valley of East Africa. Other major finds of this kind were also made at Chad, Lake Turkana in Kenya, Hadar (i.e. "Lucy") and the Awash Valley in Ethiopia, and at Sterkfontein, Swartkrans, Kromdraai and Taung in South Africa. Among recent discoveries are those in 2001 of Meave Leakey, of a 3.5–3.2 million-year-old hominid skull from the west side of Lake Turkana, and in 2006 of Tim White, of the University of California, Berkeley (who once worked with the Leakeys), who found the remains of at least eight individuals of the species *Australopithecus anamensis*, dating to 4.1 million years ago, in the Middle Awash of Ethiopia.

Africa's History

Civilization is believed to have begun in what is now the heart of the Sahara Desert, which in 5200 BC was savanna, and far less arid than it is today. Agriculture was possible, but poor soil and limited rainfall made cultivation difficult, keeping populations sparse and largely pastoral. Early populations also followed river valleys, such as the Nile, Upper Congo, and Niger. By 1500 BC agriculture had spread, domestic animals were being kept,

OPPOSITE: The Great Pyramid of Giza is the oldest and largest of the three pyramids at Giza. The Great Sphinx is in the foreground.

ABOVE: Blue-colored paint dominates the old medina in the city of Chefchaouen, Morocco.

ABOVE RIGHT: The ruins and the Roman site of Volubilis, Morocco, that date from 217 AD.

technologies such as iron-smelting were being practised, and the population was on the increase.

Africa's first great civilization emerged in Egypt in around 3200 BC, while Carthage was founded by the Phoenicians in North Africa in the 9th century BC. In 146 BC, after the Third Punic War, North Africa became part of the Roman Empire, the province comprising what is present-day northern Tunisia, as well as the Mediterranean coast of modern-day western Libya along to Syrtis Minor.

Christianity spread across these areas from Palestine via Egypt, also passing south beyond the borders of the Roman world into Nubia and by at least the 6th century into Ethiopia, where in previous centuries the Semitic Kingdom of Axum (Aksum) had flourished.

Islam spread via Spain to North Africa in the 7th century AD, reinforcing the Arab influence that

had long prevailed, and spreading to East and Central Africa where an extraordinary tribal and cultural diversity was already in existence.

By the 9th century a string of dynastic states stretched across the sub-Saharan savanna, the most powerful of them being Ghana, Gao, and the Kanem-Bornu empire, with Kanem accepting Islam in the 11th

 Even after the Sahara had returned to being a desert, it could still be penetrated by people traveling between the north and south. The use of oxen for desert crossings was common, prior to the introduction of the camel, and trade routes followed chains of oases, located at intervals across the desert.

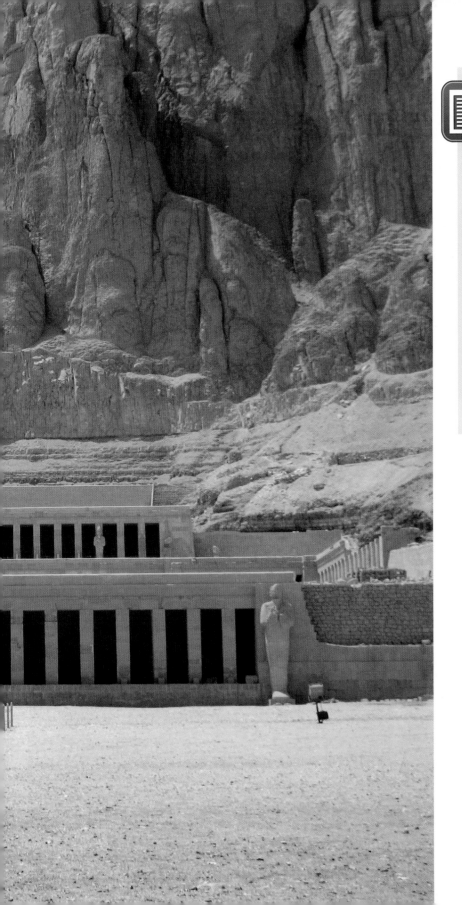

Mortuary Temple of Hatshepsut

Pictured here is the Mortuary Temple of Hatshepsut, also known as the Djeser-Djeseru "Holy of Holies." It is an ancient funerary shrine in Upper Egypt. Dedicated to the Pharaoh Hatshepsut, it is located beneath the cliffs at Deir el Bahari, on the west bank of the Nile near the Valley of the Kings. The mortuary temple is dedicated to the sun god Amun and is situated next to the mortuary temple of Mentuhotep II, which served both as an inspiration, and later, a quarry. It is considered one of the most important sites of ancient Egypt.

century. Ghana declined and was superseded by Mali, under whose empire the ancient trading cities of Djenné and Timbuktu became centers of both trade and Islamic learning.

Little is known of Africa's history in the interim, but it is recorded that Vasco da Gama explored East Africa's coast in 1498, establishing what would be centuries of European domination and exploitation.

Precolonial Africa possibly possessed as many as 10,000 states, characterized by many different kinds of political organization and rule. These included small family groups of hunter-gatherers, such as the San people of southern Africa;

larger, more structured groups, such as the Bantu-speaking people of central and southern Africa; the heavily-structured clan groups in the Horn of Africa; the large Sahelian kingdoms and autonomous city-states, such as those of the Yoruba in West Africa; and the Swahili coastal trading towns of East Africa.

Light was shed on the Dark Continent by the great explorers of the 18th–19th centuries: Mungo Park, Livingstone, Stanley, Burton, and Speke. But the harsh climate and endemic diseases made large-scale settlement unattractive to Europeans over huge areas of the continent, and West Africa came to be known as the "white man's grave." Exceptions were the area settled by the Dutch and then the British from the 17th century, now South Africa; the highlands of Kenya, settled by the British; North Africa (Algeria) by the French in the 19th and 20th centuries; and Libya by the Italians in the 20th century. The desire for colonies and the promise of acquiring rich resources then led to the Scramble for Africa in the 19th century, with Belgium, Germany, Italy, Portugal, Spain, and predominantly Britain and France, being the main protagonists.

OPPOSITE ABOVE: Djemaa el Fna Square, Marrakech, Morocco is a large public square where small merchants, hawkers, and entertainers work. It is popular with tourists and locals alike.

OPPOSITE: The Habib Bourguiba Mausoleum portico, Monastir, Tunisia.

RIGHT: The minaret and courtyard of the Great Mosque, Kairouan, Tunisia.

Text-Dependent Questions

1. What countries claim to be the origin of civilization?

2. The Sahara has not always been a desert. What was it originally?

3. Ancient populations followed three river valleys. Name the rivers?

NORTH AFRICA

The Maghreb

In modern times the Maghreb comprises the political units of Morocco, Algeria, Tunisia, Libya, and Mauritania. To the north, the region is bounded by the Mediterranean Sea, and to the west by the Atlantic Ocean, running south-west from the Straits of Gibraltar to the deserts of Mauritania. The eastern boundary is geographically open, and some medieval Arab geographers considered the Maghreb began westwards from Alexandria in Egypt, although most accepted that Egypt was in fact outside the Maghreb. Maghreb means "western" in Arabic, and was often called Barbary by the Europeans.

Words to Understand

Annexation: To incorporate a territory into an existing political unit such as a country, state, county, or city.

Predynastic: Pertaining to, or existing in the period before the rule of a given dynasty or dynasties.

Slavery: The condition in which one person is owned as property by another and is under the owner's control.

Later, the Sahara came to form an ethnic and cultural divide, with Arabs and Islam predominating along Africa's northern coast, and the lands stretching from the Atlas Mountains to the sea adopting Mediterranean influences. The Saharan interior was inhabited by Berbers and Tuaregs, while the sub-Saharan region was more ethnically diverse.

To the Sahara's south lies the Sahel (meaning "shore" or "border" in Arabic), which forms the transition between the Sahara Desert to the north and the more fertile region to the south, and which is lightly populated by pastoralists. This is a vast area of semi-arid savanna, known as the Sudan (not to be confused with the country of that name). The West Sudanian savanna runs from the Atlantic Ocean to eastern Nigeria, the East Sudanian savanna runs from the Cameroon Highlands east to the Ethiopian Highlands, extending to the tropical equatorial zone in the south.

Since travel by sea was easier than crossing the Sahara, these countries have historically had more in common with other Mediterranean lands than with Africa. They also have a different population, comprising the original

inhabitants, the Berbers; Arabs, who arrived following the rapid expansion of Islam; Jews; Iberian converts to Islam; other Europeans who had either arrived as slaves or colonialists; and Turks from the Ottoman Empire. The Ottomans ruled the area until 1834 when the French moved in.

The Maghreb was the birthplace of Tertullian (ca. 160–ca. 240) and St. Augustine of Hippo (354–430). Quintus Septimus Florens Tertullianus was born in Carthage to pagan parents, but became a Christian at some point before AD 197. His writings include Christian apologetics and attacks on pagan idolatry and Gnosticism

St. Augustine was a Berber, born in Tagaste in present-day Algeria, his mother, St. Monica, being the ideal Christian mother. Augustine was well-educated and suffered various crises, both intellectual and moral, before his commitment to Christianity. Many remember him for the quotation, "Grant me chastity, but not yet," despite the fact that he viewed lust as a mortal sin. The quotation: "Love the sinner, hate the sin" is also attributed to him. He was influenced by Platonism and developed concepts that were to become important in the history of the early Christian church, such as original sin and the concept of the "just war."

OPPOSITE: A Berber woman.

ABOVE RIGHT: A Tuareg man leading a camel in the Sahara Desert.

RIGHT: A caravan of Bedouins and camels crossing the desert.

The domination of Christianity ended when Arab invasions brought Islam to the Maghreb in 647. Carthage fell in 698, the remainder of the region following in subsequent decades. From the 8th to the 13th centuries Islam gradually spread south into West Africa, there having already been evidence that Christianity was beginning to fade during the 10th century. The Maghreb was united politically only during the first years of Arab rule, and again under the Almohads (1159–1229).

The Maghreb was deeply affected by French colonialism, which ended bitterly in Algeria in the Algerian War of Independence (1954–1962), and the Algerian Civil War (1991–99).

The Arab Maghreb Union had been established in 1989 to promote co-operation and integration among the Arab states of North Africa, its members being Algeria, Libya, Mauritania, Morocco, and Tunisia. Muammar al-Qaddafi, of Libya, originally envisioned the Mahgreb as an Arab superstate, but it is more likely to function as a North African common market. The union's progress has been hindered, however, by political unrest, especially in Algeria, and tensions over Western Sahara between Morocco and the Polisario movement based in Algeria.

BELOW: Constantine is Algeria's third largest city.

Ibn Battuta

A famous Maghrebi, and one of the most interesting of travelers was Ibn Battuta, a Muslim born in Tangier, Morocco, during the time of the Merinid Sultanate. In 1325, when he was about 20, Ibn Battuta went on the *hajj*, the pilgrimage to Mecca, but instead of returning home, went on traveling, eventually covering about 75,000 miles (117,000km) of the Islamic world and beyond (about 44 modern countries).

This is further than Marco Polo traveled and a greater journey than many people make today, despite easier travel. He eventually wrote his memoirs, aptly entitled, *A Gift to Those Who Contemplate the Wonders of Cities and the Marvels of Traveling*.

European Slavery in North Africa

Barbary or the Barbary Coast, the name having been derived from the Berber people of North Africa, was the term used by Europeans to describe the western and middle coastal regions of North Africa during the 16th–19th centuries. Today, the name evokes the pirates and slave traders based on that coast, who attacked ships and coastal settlements around the Mediterranean and North Atlantic, and captured and traded slaves taken from Europe and sub-Saharan Africa.

The four Barbary nations of North Africa – Morocco, Algiers, Tunis, and Tripoli (Libya) – had been plundering merchant shipping for

RIGHT: **A Barbary Pirate** by Pier Francesco Mola ca.1650.

BELOW: The Bombardment of Algiers, August 27, 1816 by George Chambers Sr.

In 1816 a squadron under Admiral Sir Edward Pellew was fitted out and sent to Algiers where they arrived, in company with a small Dutch squadron, on August 27, 1816. They sought the release of the British Consul, who had been detained, and over 1,000 Christian slaves, many being seamen taken by the Algerines. When they received no reply the fleet bombarded Algiers in the most spectacular of several similar punitive actions of this period that finally broke the power of the "Barbary pirates," who had been a plague on European commerce in the Mediterranean for centuries.

centuries, blackmailing foreign nations wishing to trade in African ports and sail unmolested through Mediterranean waters. They demanded tribute money, seized ships, and held crews for ransom or sold them into slavery.

During the late 1500s and early 1600s, around 35,000 European Christian slaves were held, many in Tripoli, Tunis, and various Moroccan towns, but mostly in Algiers. These were predominantly mariners, taken with their ships, but many were fishermen and villagers taken from coastal areas. Although the British captives were numerous, many more were taken from lands closer to Africa, these being Spain and Italy in particular. It is said that

the coasts of Valencia, Andalusia, Calabria, and Sicily were raided so frequently that there was eventually no one left to capture.

Some European coastal areas eventually became depopulated and the people impoverished, and the destruction in some parts of Europe was devastating. Many struggled to get enough money together to pay ransoms and get people home, though payment was frequently not honored.

In the 16th–19th centuries it is believed that between 1,000,000 and 1,250,000 Europeans were taken, which although small by comparison with the Atlantic slave trade to the Americas, was considerable nonetheless.

White slaves in Barbary were generally from poor families and, like the Africans taken to the Americas, had little hope of buying back their freedom: most would end their days dying of starvation, disease, or maltreatment.

In the waters off the Devon coast of England, at Salcombe, is the wreck of a pirate ship or *xebec*, containing the largest haul of Islamic gold discovered in British waters. Some coins had been halved, presumably so that the booty could be divided equally between the crew.

OPPOSITE: Old Algiers where the majority of European Christian slaves were kept.

BELOW: Meknes, Morocco was founded by Moulay Ismail.

Moulay Ismail (who ruled Morocco from 1672–1727) used mostly European slaves on the construction of his new capital at Meknes. Death tolls were high and his total consumption of slaves may have been several hundred thousand. He also sold slaves back to Europe for exorbitant sums.

After the American Revolution (1775–83) and independence, the United States could no longer rely on the protection of the British navy and, like other European nations, agreed to pay tribute to the Barbary states for unmolested passage into and through the Mediterranean. In May 1801, the United States refused to succumb to the increasing demands for tribute by the Pasha of Tripoli, as a result of which the First Barbary War (1801–05) was declared. While Tripoli was not a strong power, and little effort would have been necessary to blockade it, it was feared that the other Barbary powers would join in against the United States.

The Barbary Wars were mostly naval conflicts, beginning with the Tripoli conflict and later with that of Algiers (Second Barbary War 1815).

Although annual payments had been maintained to the other Barbary states, Algiers continued to seize American merchantmen, for which increased payments were demanded and secured. As a result, the United States declared war on Algiers, following which a treaty, humiliating to the once-proud piratical state, was secured, whereby no future payments would be made, all American property would be restored, Christian slaves would be emancipated, reparation would be made for a merchantman recently seized, and civilized treatment would be accorded to prisoners-of-war. Tunis and Tripoli were forced to accept equally stringent terms, and an American presence remained in

the Mediterranean, ensuring the safe progress of American commerce.

In the initial line of the Marines' hymn, "From the Halls of Montezuma to the Shores of Tripoli," Montezuma efers to the Battle of Chapultepec, during the Mexican-American War, while Tripoli refers to actions during the First Barbary War and the decisive Battle of Derna in 1805.

The Barbary slave trade continued sporadically up until the dawn of the 20th century, eventually disappearing under French rule.

The Sahara Desert

The Sahara divides the northern part of the continent into North and sub-Saharan Africa. The southern border of the Sahara is marked by a band of semi-arid savanna, known as the Sahel, while south of the Sahel lies sub-Saharan Africa's lusher Sudan and the Congo river basin.

About 5 million years ago, climate change turned the area into a desert. A further change in climate, around 5000 BC, made the area much wetter, and petroglyphs and fossils testify to human activity.

BELOW: Bizarre sandstone cliffs in the Sahara Desert, Tassili N'Ajjer, Algeria.

OPPOSITE: The Shali Fortress in Siwa Oasis is an oasis in Egypt, located between the Qattara Depression and the Egyptian Sand Sea in the Libyan Desert.

Desertification, however, set in around 3000 BC, and the area became much like it is today.

Deserts are always interesting and the scenery is far from monotonous. The Sahara comprises *hamada* (stony plateaux), gravel

plains, and salt flats, with large sand dunes forming only a minor part. The topography ranges from the Tibesti Massif of northern Chad (at 11,000 feet/3350 meters) to the Qattara Depression of Egypt (at 436 feet/133 meters). Scattered, fertile oases usually lie in depressions, punctuating the ancient caravan routes which, over time, have been adapted into modern roads. Here, water is present where the water table comes to the surface, and at greater depths lies in huge underground aquifers. These are believed to be filled with water

dating from the Pleistocene period, when the Sahara was much wetter than it is today; the more than 20 lakes or *chotts* in the north, and the areas of salt flats and boggy salt marshes, are also thought to be remnants of this pluvial age.

We know that rivers once ran through the Sahara, because dried-up riverbeds, known as *wadis*, still exist, which fill up with water and become active streams for a short time. The Nile and the Niger are the only permanent rivers in the region, being fed by rainfall outside the area.

Natural Resources

Important discoveries of minerals, oil, and gas have been made in the Sahara, but in most cases inaccessibility has delayed their exploitation. Salt is still mined, as in the past, at Taoudenni in Mali, and at Bilma in Niger, and it is transported, as in the days of the great medieval kingdoms of West Africa, by camel caravans across the desert.

Sand Dunes of Erg Chebbi

Erg Chebbi is located in the Sahara Desert. It is one of Morocco's two Saharan ergs (large seas of dunes formed by wind-blown sand). The other is Erg Chigaga near M'hamid.

The dunes reach a height of up to 492 feet (150m) in places and span an area of 31 miles (50km) from north to south and up to 6 miles (10km) from east to west lining the Algerian border.

MEDITERRANEAN SEA

Beirut
LEBANON
Damascus
SYRIA

Baghdad

IRAQ

Jerusalem
ISRAEL
JORDAN
Amman

Alexandria

Tanta
Gizeh
Cairo
Helwan
Bani Suwaif
Al-Minya

KUV

SAUDI ARABIA

Asyut
Sohag
Qena
Nile
Luxor

EGYPT

Assuan

Lake
Nasser

RED

SEA

Atbara

Nile

SUDAN

Atbara

Atbara

ERITREA

Asmara

Sana
YI

Omdurman
Al-Chartum Bahri
Khartoum

White Nile
Kusti
Blue Nile

Lake
Tana

DJIBOUTI
Djibouti

Bahr al-Ghazal
Malakal
Sobat
Blue Nile

RAL
N REP.

White Nile/Bar al-Dschabal

SOUTH SUDAN

Addis Ababa

ETHIOPIA

Juba

Lake
Turkana

SOMA

OCRATIC REP.
THE CONGO

Albert Nile
Lake
Albert
Lake Kyoga
UGANDA

KENYA

INL

Kampala

Lake
Edward
Lake
Victoria
Nairobi

OC

Lake
Kivu
RWANDA
Kigali

BURUNDI
Bujumbura
★ Source of the Nile
TANZANIA

The Nile and its Tributaries

The River Nile has two major tributaries, the White Nile and the Blue Nile, the former being the longer of the two, while the latter is the source of most of the Nile's water and fertile soil.

The northern section of the Nile flows almost entirely through desert, from Sudan into Egypt, a country whose civilization depended on the river in ancient times. Most of the population of Egypt, and all of its cities, with the exception of those near to the coast, lie along those parts of the Nile valley north of Aswan, and nearly all the cultural and historical sites of ancient Egypt are to be found along its banks. The Nile ends in a large delta that empties into the Mediterranean Sea.

During the Neolithic era, several **predynastic** cultures developed independently in Upper and Lower Egypt. A unified kingdom was founded in around 3150 BC by King Menes, giving rise to a series of dynasties that ruled Egypt for the next three millennia, the Nile valley kingdoms reaching their apogee from about 2700–1087 BC. These kingdoms produced some of the world's most celebrated monuments, including the pyramids of the Giza Plateau and its Great Sphinx, and the numerous ancient artifacts of the southern city of

LEFT: Map showing the river Nile from its source to the Mediterranean Sea.

OPPOSITE ABOVE: The Temple of Philae at Aswan on the banks of the Nile.

OPPOSITE BELOW: Lush vegetation on the banks of the Nile.

Luxor, such as the Karnak Temple and the Valley of the Kings.

Today, what was once the ancient land of Nubia is divided between Egypt and the Republic of the Sudan. In ancient times Nubia, also known as Kush or the Southern Lands, was the territory below the First Cataract of the Nile, and during the Greco-Roman period in Egypt was part of Ethiopia. Nubia was important to Egypt as early as the 1st dynasty, and Egypt was to plunder Nubia many times for her bountiful natural resources.

Egypt, however, was never fully in control of Nubia, and during Egypt's Third Intermediate Period Nubia invaded Egypt itself, and several Nubians became pharaohs of Egypt's 25th dynasty.

Nubian rule was established in the northern part of Sudan in about 300 BC and the kingdom lasted for 900 years, being predominantly Christian until the 14th century.

Today the modern inhabitants of southern Egypt and northern Sudan still refer to themselves as Nubians, speaking the Nubian language as well as Arabic. Nubia was the homeland of Africa's earliest black culture, with a history that can be traced from 3100 BC onward through its monuments and artifacts, also through the written records of the Egyptians and the Greeks and Romans who subsequently came to rule in Egypt.

A dam was constructed at Aswan, Egypt, in the 1960s, creating the 500- mile-long Lake Nasser, which permanently flooded ancient temples and tombs as well as hundreds of modern villages in Sudan. While the dam was under construction, hundreds of

archeologists worked in Egypt and Sudan to excavate as many ancient sites as possible.

Muhammad Ali, although Turkish-born, was pasha and viceroy of Egypt from 1805–48 and the founder of the dynasty that ruled Egypt from the beginning of the 19th century to the middle of the 20th. He was no Egyptian nationalist, however, but sought to further his own ambitions to gain power in the eastern Mediterranean. Egypt was important for what it could do for him, and yet his efforts to unify, strengthen, and modernize Egypt made him one of the country's greatest rulers.

Born in 1830, Ismail was governor and then khedive of Egypt from 1863–1879, after his predecessor, Said, died, Ismail being the eldest male in the family and according to Egypt's rule the next in line. He displayed some of his grandfather Mohammad Ali's enthusiasm for modernization, and Ismail's ambitions extended to seeking independence from Ottoman administration. Through bribing those with influence, he was able to obtain the Sultan's approval to restrict ruling succession to his own descendants, gaining the title of khedive in 1867.

Ismail opposed the slave trade in Sudan, expanded Egypt's properties in Africa, and inaugurated the Suez Canal for international navigation, that was opened in 1869. During his reign, however, Egypt's debts began to mount, allowing England and France to interfere in Egypt's internal affairs under the guise of protecting its interests.

Under pressure from the two powers, Sultan Abd El-Hamid II isolated Ismail, due to his poor financial policy in 1879, and Ismail's son, Tawfik, succeeded him as Khedive of Egypt.

Tawfik Pasha had plans for a great African nation but ran into severe financial problems, resulting in the British invasion of Egypt in 1882, which affected the way Africa was divided in the following years.

Sudan had its own religious teachers and did not appreciate interference from Egypt. The Mahdi (Messiah), Muhammad Ahmed, a religious leader in Sudan, who had proclaimed himself the prophesied redeemer of Islam who would appear at the end of time, in 1881 declared a *jihad*, raised an army, and led a successful religious war to topple the Egyptian occupation of Sudan. Under his religious authority the divided clans of the Baggara and their subject Fur tribesmen were united in an alliance dedicated to establishing an Islamic state as the first step towards universal Islam.

The Mahdi is remembered mostly for the death of General Gordon at Khartoum. He himself died shortly afterwards and his successor established a strong secular state, which was not quite what the Mahdi had planned, and Sudan was retaken by British-Egyptian forces.

LEFT: The Aswan High Dam provides irrigation for crops and hydroelectricity.

OPPOSITE ABOVE: Ships passing through the Suez Canal.

The Kingdom of Axum ruled from the 1st century AD, and at its height controlled northern Ethiopia, Eritrea, northern Sudan, southern Egypt, Djibouti, Yemen, and southern Saudi Arabia. Axum was converted to Christianity in the 4th century, and its people carved churches in rocks and wrote and interpreted religious texts. It was and is the alleged resting place of the Ark of the Covenant and the home of the Queen of Sheba.

Axum was an important marketplace for ivory, which was exported throughout the ancient world; it controlled two harbors on the Red Sea: Adulis, near Massawa, and Avalites (Assab).

Between 1855 and 1889, Ethiopia (Axum having adopted the name in the 4th century) began to make its presence felt. It was different from other African states in that it had a central institution in the ancient Coptic Church which, being an educator, provided an elite of like-minded people able to deal with Europeans. A succession of rulers was able to control and extend the state and, more importantly, were skillful enough to avoid the financial and diplomatic problems that might lead to European intervention.

In 1896, under Emperor Menelik II, the Ethiopians were able to resist the Italians at the Battle of Adwa, thus preventing their attempts at conquest. Ethiopia was brutally occupied by Mussolini's Italy from 1936 to 1941, a period which ended with its liberation by British Empire and Ethiopian patriot forces. By 1914, Ethiopia and Liberia were the only independent states still existing in Africa.

In 1952 Haile Selassie orchestrated Ethiopia's federation with Eritrea, which he dissolved in 1962, Eritrea's **annexation** sparking the Eritrean War of Independence. Although Haile Selassie was seen as a national and African hero, opinion within Ethiopia turned against him due to the worldwide oil crisis of 1973, food shortages, uncertainty regarding the succession, border wars, and discontent among the middle classes.

Haile Selassie's reign came to an end in 1974, when a Soviet-backed Marxist-Leninist military junta, the "Derg," led by Mengistu Haile Mariam, deposed him and established a one-party Communist state.

Text-Dependent Questions

1. Explain the meaning of Maghreb and the countries it consists of?

2. How many Barbary wars were there?

3. What permanent rivers run through the Sahara Desert?

4. What year was the Suez Canal opened?

WEST AFRICA

Complex societies inhabited the mid-Niger and Senegal valleys from about 200 BC. Trade across the Sahara enabled the development of great empires, the best-known of these being Ghana, Mali, and Songhai.

The Ghana Empire, ca. 750–1076
The first and largest of the great medieval empires in West Africa, the Ghana **empire**, as Europe and Arabia referred to it, on account of the title of its emperor, was known to its own citizens, a Mandé subgroup known as the Soninke, as Wagadou, reaching the height of its power in about 1000 AD.

Words to Understand

Empire: An extensive group of states or countries ruled over by a single monarch.

Ethnic: Relating to races or large groups of people who have the same customs, religion, origin, etc.

Mandinka: A West African ethnic group living mainly in Senegal, Gambia, and Sierra Leone.

The Soninke were mixed farmers, raising animals and growing millet in an area that is now south-eastern Mauritania, western Mali, and eastern Senegal. Within their territory were gold mines and the rich floodplains of the Niger river. The empire came into being due to changes in the economy of the Sahel, which allowed more

centralized states to form, and the introduction of the camel, which preceded Islam, brought about a gradual revolution in trade; for the first time, the extensive gold, ivory, and salt resources of the region could be sent north and east to

OPPOSITE: Traditional paddleboats are still used in Ghana today.

ABOVE: The Larabanga Mosque is a historic mosque, built in the Sudanese architectural style, in the village of Larabanga, Ghana. It is the oldest mosque in the country and one of the oldest in West Africa.

population centers in North Africa, the Middle East, and Europe, in exchange for manufactured goods.

Trade made the Ghana empire rich, making it famous in Africa as the "Land of Gold." Not only did it have a monopoly over its well-concealed gold mines, but it is also said to have possessed sophisticated methods of administration and taxation, also large armies, being among the first, apart from Egypt and Sudan, to build stone settlements with street layouts, walls, and buildings.

Ghana's importance faded towards the end of the 11th century when its power was crushed, after a

long struggle, by the Moroccan Almoravids, who justified the war as an act of conversion through military arms (lesser jihad), when it was in fact a bid for control of the coveted trans-Saharan trade routes. In 1076, the Almoravids captured the capital, bringing to an end the Ghana empire while converting many to Islam. Almoravid rule did not last for long and in 1087 power was returned to much weakened Soninke rule, which fell prey, in around 1140, to the rabidly anti-Muslim Sosso people, who also annexed the neighboring **Mandinka** state of Kangaba, from which the new Mali empire would arise.

The Mali Empire, 1235–1645

The Mali empire was created by another Mandé group, the Mandinka, and developed from the state of Kangaba on the upper Niger river, whose inhabitants acted as middlemen in the ancient Ghanaian gold trade. Its boundaries extended to the Hausa people in the east and to the Fulani and Tukulor peoples in the west.

In 1235, a legendary figure, Sundiata Keïta, established a federation of Mandinka tribes, which developed into an empire ruling millions of people from **ethnic** groups all over West Africa. It became immensely rich, and Mali continued to expand in the 14th century when it absorbed Gao and Timbuktu.

Mali was the second and most powerful of the African empires and a model of its kind, exerting profound cultural influences and fostering the spread of its laws and customs along the Niger river. It stretched from the Atlantic to the upper reaches of the Niger and Senegal rivers, and was able to trade gold and luxuries over a wide area, from the Atlantic to the forests of the south, up through the Sahara and far to the east.

By the 14th century, its capital, the city of Timbuktu, was the jewel in the crown not only of the Mali empire but also of the whole of West Africa. It was famous for the wealth of its rulers, and one of them, Mansa Musa, is said to have taken with him, on the *hajj* to Mecca, an impressive 180 tons of gold. Scholars and artisans were attracted to Mali, and Islam flourished; Timbuktu would have its ancient universities, while Djenné would become pivotal to Mali's trade.

The end came as a result of intrigues and struggles for the succession, which weakened the state and eventually led to revolts. The Songhai empire emerged from a Mali vassal state, became independent, and ultimately eclipsed the Mali empire.

BELOW: Traditional mud houses of the Dogon people, an ethnic group living in the central plateau region of Mali, near the city of Bandiagara, in the Mopti region.

OPPOSITE: A market in Djenné, Mali.

The Songhai Empire, 1375–1591

The Songhai were closely related to the Mandé and together they were dominant in the Songhai empire. It was from one of Mali's former conquests, Gao, that the last major empire would emerge. Although Gao had been occupied by a Songhai dynasty prior to being conquered by Mansa Musa's forces in 1325, and was its capital city, it was not until much later that the Songhai empire would emerge. It began to rise in 1464 when it conquered much of the weakening Mali empire's territory, including the cities of Timbuktu and Djenné, reaching its zenith under the Askia dynasty (1492–1592), its first ruler having been the devoutly Muslim Mohammed Touré, known as Askia the Great.

As with all empires, Songhai eventually declined. Mansur of Morocco, wishing to take control of the gold trade, sent a force armed with guns against Songhai's more primitive weapons; but governing so vast an empire began to prove irksome for the Moroccans, causing them to relinquish control of the region, leaving it to splinter into dozens of smaller kingdoms. Other states formed, but were not comparable with the empires; the Wolof established themselves in what is now Senegal, and the Hausa created important city states.

Eminent Arab geographers and historians, as well as African scholars, wrote of the empires of Ghana, Mali, Songhai and Kanem Bornu, and spoke of the famous trade routes used by these peoples, describing Ghana, as early as the 11th century, as a highly advanced and prosperous society.

The Hausa City State

The 14 Hausa kingdoms or states, comprising the "Hausa Seven" and the "Bastard Seven," were located in what would become northern Nigeria, emerging in the 13th century as vibrant trading centers in competition with Kanem-Bornu and Mali. Except for minor alliances, they functioned independently, and being rivals were never centralized into a single state. Enriched by a further eastward shift in trade, they blossomed in the late 1500s, and cities like Kano, Katsina, and Zinder remain important centers of trade.

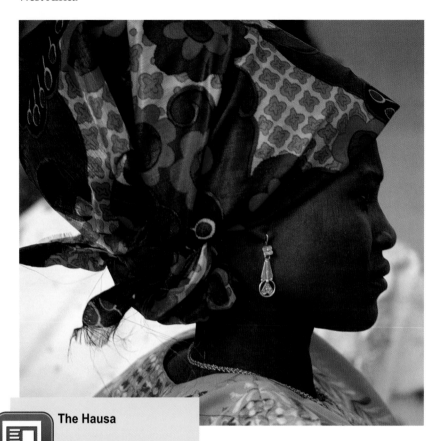

The Hausa

A Hausa woman in Nigeria. The modern Hausa of Nigeria are mainly concentrated in the provinces of Kano, Katsina, Sokoto, and Zaria, their population probably numbering between 6 and 8 million in Nigeria alone. The Hausa language is an important lingua franca in West Africa.

Although the vast majority of its inhabitants were Muslim by the 16th century, they were attacked by Muslim Fulani jihadists in the early 19th century, when the last Hausa state was finally incorporated into the Sokoto Caliphate.

Islam

Islam reached the Sahel in the 8th century, when the written history of West Africa begins. It was accepted as early as 850 in the Kingdom of Tekrur, situated on both banks of the Senegal river, whose subjects were the first indigenous people to accept Islam.

Islam arrived via traders from the Maghreb, becoming a personal faith rather than a state ideology. It became a religion largely of the rulers, while their subjects intermingled Islam with traditional beliefs. Islam then declined among the ruling classes and non-Islamic rule became common, a situation that continued until the revivalist and reform movement of the 18th century. Beginning as early as the 17th and 18th centuries, but mainly in the 19th century, the Fulani, reputed to be a people of Semitic origin, launched jihads, and took control of various West African states.

The Yoruba States

The Yoruba make up approximately 21 per cent of Nigeria's total population, and around 30 million individuals throughout West Africa.

There were seven Yoruba states, including the Oyo kingdom, Ife, and Benin, the people being non-Bantu Kwa speakers. These states had elected monarchs, some more dictatorial than others, but which were removable, while in the 18th century there were instances of rule by councils of eminent citizens. It was a sophisticated society, with the military wielding power, and guilds, societies, clubs, and religious groups providing social control. The cities were wealthy and there was patronage of the arts, the people excelling in wood carving, metalwork (especially brass), pottery, weaving, beadwork, and the production of masks.

Benin, between 1300–1850, was a wonderfully complex Yoruban

OPPOSITE: Statue of King Béhanzin in Abomey, Benin. Béhanzin (1844–1906) is considered the eleventh King of Dahomey, modern-day Benin.

state in present-day Nigeria. There were ancient walls 60-feet (18-m) high surrounding the city, which stretched for about 750 miles (1200 km), and various other constructions suggested there was a large and organized population. Stable and balanced government was created by Oba Ewuare in the 15th century, when the city was divided between the court and an area for craftsmen, who produced the celebrated bronze and brass castings that became a speciality of the kingdom. A bas relief from the palace has been likened to the Bayeux Tapestry in France.

The first contact with Europeans was by the Portuguese in 1472, followed soon after by visits to Benin city itself for the purpose of trade. This was initially in pepper and ivory, but there was a more lucrative trade in slaves, traded directly from Benin and via the island of São Tomé.

The power of Benin was ended in the 19th century when British troops destroyed the capital, the break-up of the Oyo empire having already destabilized the surrounding states

Abomey (in present-day Benin) was the capital of the ancient Kingdom of Dahomey, its royal palaces being a group of earthen structures built by the Fon people between the mid-17th and late-19th centuries, and now a UNESCO World Heritage Site.

The Atlantic slave trade, a crucial element in the so-called three-cornered trade between Europe, West Africa, and the Americas, grew and flourished between about 1500 and 1800 into a forced migration of at least 11 million people. It is impossible to over-emphasize what the removal of this number of able-bodied people did to the economy of West Africa, affecting the Yoruba states as it did all other parts of the region.

The Ashanti

Located, during the 17th–19th centuries, in the area of modern Ghana, the Ashanti was the largest and most powerful of a series of linguistically connected Akan states, which used their wealth to buy slaves from Europeans and other Africans, the first European involvement having been the trade in selling Africans to other Africans. The slaves were put to work panning for gold and in the gold mines, and were used to clear dense areas of forest. The Akan had once been hunter-gatherers, but with the clearing of the forest took to farming, growing traditional crops, such as yams and rice, and later new crops imported from America – maize and cassava (manioc) among other useful plants – which allowed them to feed the by now greatly increased population.

The Ashanti are famous for their myths, especially the stories about Anansi, who is a spider or a human being, or perhaps somewhere between the two. The legend of the "Golden Stool" is central to Ashanti nationhood, as it is believed to contain the spirit or soul of the Ashanti people. The Governor of the Gold Coast, Sir Frederick Hodgson, demanded to sit on the stool in 1900, outraging the Ashanti, after which they prepared for war.

The Ashanti traded with the Portuguese, who had built their first fort in tropical Africa in 1482, on what became known as the Gold Coast. The Ashanti were skilled metalworkers, who became famous for their lost-wax method of casting.

The purpose of the Ashanti state was to control the gold trade, among others, as well as farming.

The Ashanti had exported slaves throughout their history, but with the abolition of the slave trade were forced to rework their entire economy.

The Ashanti

The Ashanti was one of the few African states to offer serious resistance to European colonizers. Between 1823 and 1896, Britain fought four wars against the Ashanti kings (the Anglo-Ashanti Wars). In 1900, the British finally defeated the Ashanti state and incorporated it into the Gold Coast colony. Today the Ashanti are dominant in West Africa, being better educated and richer than other groups.

The Arrival of the Europeans

Throughout the 15th century, the Portuguese had been exploring Africa's coast, establishing trading posts for several types of commodities, ranging from gold to slaves, as they looked for a route to India and its spices. They were also hoping to convert the people to Christianity, making them their allies against Islam. By 1475 they had reached the Bight of Benin, and it has been suggested that the Portuguese enabled intra-African trade by shipping goods from port to port. This may have weakened the Songhai empire, however, as trade took to the sea and difficult journeys overland were abandoned.

The Portuguese were joined by other seafaring empires, profoundly affecting indigenous trade across the Sahara. Now that the direction of trade had turned towards the sea, inland states declined as coastal ones gained in wealth and power, now helped by the availability of firearms. Now the slave trade began to increase its momentum; the Portuguese needed workers on their plantations in Brazil and as other European powers established colonies in the Americas, the need for labor grew, causing the vicious trade to expand. Coastal African states began to attack their neighbors, taking captives who were then sold into slavery.

OPPOSITE: Carved stamps are used to print symbols on traditional Adinkra cloth made by the Ashanti people in Ghana.

ABOVE: African slaves processing sugar cane on the Caribbean island of Hispaniola. Engraving by Theodor de Bry (1528–1598).

The Atlantic Slave Trade

Human bondage existed in Africa since earliest times, often in the forms of agricultural labor and conscripted soldiers. Africans became part of the Atlantic trade in slaves after the European Age of Exploration, from which comes the modern Western perception of African-descended slaves owned by non-African slave traders. Africa's involvement in this trade emerged when suitable ships made it possible for long voyages to be made from the Mediterranean, down the coast of Africa, and ultimately across the Atlantic to the Americas. Before they even boarded ship, many slaves had already made long inland journeys, and had often been bought and sold several times along the way.

Slavery existed in the Americas prior to European colonization, in that the indigenous population often took and held members of other tribes captive, human sacrifice of captives being common in Aztec society. The Spanish followed by enslaving indigenous Caribbean tribes, and as the native populations declined, mostly through European diseases, came to be replaced by commercially imported Africans.

These were primarily obtained from their African homelands by coastal tribes, who captured and sold them, receiving guns and gun powder in exchange. The total slave trade to islands in the Caribbean, Brazil, Mexico and to the United States is estimated to have involved 12 million Africans, of whom 645,000 were brought to what is now the United States. In addition to African slaves, poor Europeans were brought over in substantial numbers as indentured servants, particularly in the British 13 colonies.

The European slavers were unable to capture the Africans themselves, having no desire to venture inland. Europeans rarely entered Africa's interior, due to fear of disease and fierce African resistance. They could not afford to make enemies of their suppliers, so they confined themselves to visiting marketplaces, examining prospective slaves and shipping them out.

Most of the slaves were adult males, as Africans tended to retain their females, in that they were useful for domestic and agricultural work and childbearing, while children were not economical, the cost of shipping them being the same as for an adult, while the prices that could be commanded for them were substantially less.

The Atlantic crossing took 25 to 60 days, depending on the wind and where the boat was headed, and about 16 percent of slaves died in transit. The trade in slaves peaked in the late 18th century, when the largest number of slaves were captured on raiding expeditions into the interior of West Africa. These forays were typically made by coastal African states against weaker African tribes and peoples. These mass slavers included the Oyo empire (Yoruba), the Kong empire, the kingdoms of Benin, Dahomey, Fouta Djallon, Fouta Tooro, Koya, Khasso, Kaabu, and the Fante and Ashanti confederacies.

During the 1790s, the Abolitionist movement gathered strength in England and later in America, with calls for the ending of slavery and the repatriation of slaves to Africa.

The Parliamentary campaign against the slave trade was led by William Wilberforce, who expressed his feelings with clarity and forcefulness: "Never, never will we desist, until we have wiped away this scandal from the Christian name, released ourselves from the load of guilt, under which we at present labor, and extinguished every trace of this bloody traffic, of which our posterity, looking back to the history of these enlightened times, will scarce believe that it has been suffered to exist so long a disgrace and dishonor to this country."

The British abolished the transatlantic slave trade in 1807, although it remained legal to own a slave. To some West African states,

LEFT: William Wilberforce (1759-1833). Engraved by E. Scriven.

OPPOSITE: Although founded by freed American and Caribbean slaves, Liberia is mostly inhabited by indigenous Africans, with slaves' descendants comprising 4 percent of the population.

abolition came as a heavy blow; it had been a profitable business, but it had also resulted in increased local slavery leading to rebellions. Weak rule, moreover, made former African kingdoms unable to resist imperial incursions into their territory.

The British were serious about stopping the trade and from 1808–1860 deployed a unit of the British navy, known as the West Africa Squadron, which captured 1,600 slave ships and released 150,000 Africans, while the U.S. Navy captured 24 vessels. This turned out to be an expensive exercise, costing more than British trade with Africa was worth; it was also expensive in terms of manpower as many men were lost to disease.

Text-Dependent Questions

1. What precious metal was mined to make the Ghana Empire very wealthy?

2. What is the name of the famous stool revered by the Ashanti people?

3. What is the name of the movement which arose in England and later in the United States to call a stop to the slave trade?

EAST AFRICA

The Swahili Civilization and Coastal Trade

Monsoon wind patterns facilitated trade across the Indian Ocean, carrying vessels from Africa to the Gulf, to India and back again, which led to the development of the East African ports.

Swahili, the lingua franca of East Africa, was a development of the Bantu language with European, Indian, and Arabic influences.

In 1000–1500, trading cities ran down the East African coast, from Mogadishu in present-day Somalia to Sofala (Nova Sofala) in Mozambique, which traded inland with Great Zimbabwe, while prominent ports were located on the islands of Kilwa Kisiwani, Lamu, and Paté, located in the Indian Ocean close to the southern coast of Tanzania. The Moroccan, Ibn Battuta, passed through Mombasa and Kilwa on his remarkable

Words to Understand

Lucrative: Something that produces profits, money, or wealth.

Missionary: A person sent on a religious mission, especially one sent to promote Christianity in a foreign country.

Sultan: A ruler of a Muslim country, especially of the former Ottoman Empire.

journey in 1331, providing the first accurate accounts of the flourishing Muslim cities of the Swahili.

Kilwa (Quiloa to the Portuguese) dates to AD 800 and was a major center of trade, being the most prominent of about 35 trading posts on the Indian Ocean. It was important during the Shirazi dynasty of the 11th and 12th centuries, when a great mosque was

built under the rule of Ali al-Hasan, and trade connections with southern Africa and the Near and Far East were established. Kilwa was the major exchange point for gold, ivory, iron, and coconuts from the kingdom of the Mwene Mutabe, jewellery and textiles from India, and porcelain from China. The first gold coins struck south of the Sahara, after the decline of Axum, were minted here, one of which was found south of the Zambezi river.

LEFT: Modern Mogadishu in Somalia was part of an ancient trade route.

OPPOSITE LEFT: Kilwa Kisiwani was a settlement on an island off the southern coast of present-day Tanzania in eastern Africa. Historically, it was the center of the Kilwa Sultanate, a medieval sultanate whose authority at its height in the 13th–15th centuries AD stretched the entire length of the Swahili Coast. Kilwa Kisiwani has been designated a UNESCO World Heritage Site.

OPPOSITE: An early 20th century portrait of Pedro Ávares Cabral.

Arab Slavery

The Arab slave trade began from about the 7th century onward, with slaves being transported across the Sahara to North Africa and across East Africa to Zanzibar, Dar es Salaam and Mombasa. The Sultan of Oman moved his capital to Mombasa in 1837, where he set about expanding the trade.

Some 11–17 million slaves crossed the Red Sea and Indian Ocean between 650 and 1900. Notable among these were the black eunuchs, provided for the Ottoman sultans to guard their harems, who were brought from Ethiopia and Sudan. Each **sultan** could have 200––400 eunuchs, the chief among them having immense influence and huge wealth, being the third in importance at court after the sultan himself. Unlike the Atlantic trade, slaves taken from East Africa were mainly women and boys, the descendants of whom can be found living in India and Pakistan today.

European Intervention

Kilwa's fortunes changed in the late 15th century when the Portuguese explorer, Pedro Álvares Cabral, visited Kilwa and reported seeing beautiful houses made of coral. In 1502 the Portuguese established full control of the island, their intention being to capture the **lucrative** Indian Ocean spice trade. Kilwa began to decline because of Portuguese activity, but in 1587 marauders from the Zambezi valley, armed only with spears, massacred everyone in the town. The Omani Arabs of Paté managed to dislodge the Portuguese from their part of the coast in 1698, but Portuguese remained in Mozambique until the late 20th century.

David Livingstone (1813–1873)

David Livingstone, the Scottish **missionary** and explorer, witnessed the slaughter of villagers by slave traders at a village on the Lualaba river, a headstream of the Congo, leading him to send home a letter describing the event, which so infuriated the public as to cause the British government to pressure the Sultan of Zanzibar to stop the trade, which was only partially successful. At home, Livingstone continued to publicize the horrors of the slave trade. He also secured private support for another expedition to Africa to look for the source of the Nile and make a further report on slavery. This lasted from 1866 until Livingstone's death in 1873.

ABOVE: Explorer and missionary, David Livingstone.

RIGHT: Stone Town in Zanzibar. Zanzibar was part of the slave route.

INLAND AFRICA

The Bantu

The Bantu are an ethnic and linguistic group, numbering about 120 million, which apart from the extreme south-west, inhabits most of the African continent south of the Congo river. Few cultural generalizations can be made as far as the Bantu are concerned, and the classification is primarily linguistic, there being almost 100 Bantu languages, including Luganda, Zulu, and Swahili.

The origins of the Bantu are believed to lie in Cameroon. In about 1000 BC, the Bantu began a diaspora that was probably one of the largest in human history, and which possibly continued until the

Words to Understand

Diaspora: The dispersion or spread of any people from their original homeland.

Expulsion: The action or process of forcing someone to leave a place.

Status-conscious: Aware or excessively interested in one's social status.

3rd or 4th centuries AD. One group went east and south into Zimbabwe, Mozambique, and southern Africa and another turned west towards Angola, Namibia, and north-

western Botswana, the first becoming the Shona, Xhosa, Kikuyu, and Zulu, noted for their large herds of cattle, while the western **diaspora** include the

Herero and Tonga people, famous for their metalworking skills.

Before the European conquest of Africa, Bantu tribes tended to be either pastoral and warlike or

OPPOSITE: Ugandan farmland. The Bantu state of Buganda is in present-day Uganda.

ABOVE: Two Masai warriors clad in traditional scarlet clothing. Today this tribe mainly inhabits southern Kenya and northern Tanzania.

agricultural and peaceful, and there were some highly developed Bantu states, including Buganda in present-day Uganda. Possibly through fear of European encroachment, several additional Bantu states developed in the 19th century, notably among the Zulu and the Sotho.

The Bantu-speakers of modern Kenya are the agriculturalist Kikuyu, the largest group in the country, while possibly the best known are the Nilotic pastoral and nomadic Masai, the tall, scarlet-clad

warriors and tenders of cattle. The Masai have always been jealous of their particular way of life: they never condoned slavery, and their dislike of eating game and birds meant that fewer species disappeared from Masai territories than elsewhere, and are often where game reserves are now sited.

Early archeologists found it hard to believe that such complex sites and organizations could be indigenous to Africa, particularly that of Great Zimbabwe. Subsequent work was intended to validate

historical interpretation of oral traditions, but more recent archeological surveys have stuck to evaluating the evidence as it stands. Oral traditions in Africa often attempt to explain origins and account for earthworks and other such sites.

Bantu-speaking people with pronounced ideas of social and political organization, known as the Cwezi, came into south-west Uganda in around 500 BC, where they lived by agriculture, metalworking, and pottery. By the 14th century, complex and advanced states had developed between Lake Victoria and Lake Edward, the ancient Kitara empire extending over modern Uganda and northern Tanzania, but was weakened when it was invaded by the Nilotic Luo people from Sudan. Successor states included the kingdoms of Bachwezi, Bunyoro, Ankole, and Buganda, all of which were in Uganda.

OPPOSITE: The Cwezi people lived near Lake Victoria.

BELOW: The Kitara empire reached as far north as Tanzania. This is Mount Kilimanjaro.

Bunyoro was the largest state in the area in the 16th–17th centuries, ruled by a kabaka (king) and extending from Rwanda to Tanzania. Unlike the West African states, Bunyoro was a cattle-based society,

and also benefited from its control of some of the holiest shrines in the region, with more of its wealth coming from salt production, metalworking, and control of lucrative trade routes.

Ankole Watusi Cattle

The Ankole were a Cwezi people, notable for developing the Ankole Watusi breed of cattle. The breed is instantly recognizable due to its massive horns. Being a local breed, the cattle are well-adapted to thrive on impoverished grassland with little available water.

The Omugabe of Ankole ruled over a complex **status-conscious** society, the cattle-owning elite being at the top of the pile. The Kingdom of Toro, an offshoot of the Ankole, was developed in about 1880 by a breakaway group.

Buganda differed from Bunyoro and Ankole in keeping fewer cattle but also growing crops. A vassal state of Bunyoro, Buganda came to the fore in the 18th and 19th centuries, making forays over a wide area in its search for cattle, ivory, and slaves, and trading with the coastal Muslims from about 1840. By this means Bunyoro was able to acquire

BELOW: Long-horned Ankole Watusi cattle in Rwanda.

OPPOSITE: The Nairobi to Mombasa train on the historic Uganda "Lunatic" railway line in Tsavo National Park, Kenya.

firearms, enabling it to challenge Buganda, but with little success.

Buganda became the centerpiece of the Protectorate of Uganda, allowing it to benefit from its useful alliance with the British. By the time of Ugandan independence in 1962, the Bugandans had the highest standard of living and were the best

educated and most literate group in the land.

In an interesting twist on the slave trade (for indentured labor was virtually the same thing), 32,000 Indians were imported to build the "lunatic line," as detractors called it, this being the railway from Mombasa to Kisumu on the eastern side of Lake Victoria, not the least of their problems being the man-eating lions of Tsavo, which had to be shot before work could proceed. The work was carried out between 1896 and 1901 and replaced ox carts, the previous means of transport. The railway was costly, however, and made no economic sense. The Asians were subsequently involved in the development of towns, and with the surge in trade that followed in the wake of these developments, were able to set up businesses, homes, temples, and other institutions, some of them becoming rich in the process. In the early 1920s, serious discussions began between the British and Indian authorities with regard to making East Africa a colony of India. There are still large numbers of Indian residents here, as well as in southern Africa, despite Idi Amin's **expulsion** of them from Uganda in 1972.

Text-Dependent Questions

1. What country did the Bantu people originally come from?

2. What name is given to the the tall scarlet-dressed tribesmen and where do they mainly live today?

3. What is the nickname of the historic railroad that was built through Uganda and who built it?

SOUTHERN AFRICA

From the 7th–11th centuries, Bantu migrants reached southern Africa, where they were to form great city states. Great Zimbabwe was at its height between the 11th and the mid-15th centuries when, for reasons unknown, it was abandoned. It had impressive stone buildings, built by the ancestors of the Shona, the wealth of whose empire came from large-scale gold and copper mining, these metals, together with iron and ivory, having been traded since the 10th century. Their control extended over the area between the Zambezi and Limpopo rivers and extended west as far as the Kalahari Desert.

There were other local cities, Khami being a 15th-century

BELOW: The Zambezi river.

OPPOSITE ABOVE: The Kalahari Desert.

OPPOSITE BELOW: A family sitting outside their traditional house in a village on the edge of the Kalahari Desert.

settlement with large stone structures, while Dhlo-Dhlo, which flourished in the 17th–18th centuries, was a town of some importance; all traded with the coastal Kilwa and Sofala Arabs.

Groups of eastern Bantu came to southern Africa, where there were immense areas for them to occupy, which allowed them to spread without forming centralized states. There were also Nguni peoples in the area, among them Swazis, Zulus, and Xhosas, who despite having chieftains failed to develop large urban and political structures; this was because groups tended to split when they became too large to handle. They became the Swazi and Zulu "nations" in the 19th century.

Words to Understand

Humanitarian: Concerned with or seeking to promote human welfare.

Indigenous: Originating or occurring naturally in a particular place (native).

Migrants: People who move from one place to another in order to find work or better living conditions.

BELOW: A Bas-relief panel on the Voortrekker Monument, near Pretoria, South Africa. It depicts the exodus of farmers from the eastern Cape colony, 1836–37, known as the Great Trek.

OPPOSITE: Depiction of a Zulu attack on a Boer camp in February 1838, known as the Weenen Massacre.

The Boers

The Boers, Dutch farmers who were hungry for land, had been moving inland ever since the Cape Colony of what is now South Africa was established by the Dutch East India Company in 1652. By the time the British seized the colony in 1795, the Dutch had gradually acquired all the land of the **indigenous** Khoikhoi, many of whom were killed, died of smallpox, or become herdsmen to the colonists. The Dutch government passed a law in 1787 subjecting the remaining nomadic Khoikhoi to certain restrictions, which either made them more dependent upon the farmers or compelled them to migrate northwards, facing the hostility of their old foe, the Bushmen, which the Boers were already hunting down.

When the British tried to enforce a **humanitarian** native policy in the 1830s, the stubbornly independent Boers trekked further into the boundless interior, where they clashed with other fiercer African people of Bantu stock, and suffered an appalling massacre at the hands

The Zulus

In 1818–28, the warrior leader, Shaka Zulu, unified his people and turned them into a powerful fighting force, moving against other Africans and Europeans in South Africa. Shaka's organization was something previously unknown in Africa, being a powerful, centralized militaristic kingdom. The army had around 40,000 men, organized by age and segregated from society, with women and old men doing the work of the villages. Shaka's army was successful because it trained hard and was disciplined in the use of short, stabbing spears as well as long assegais.

After his mother's death in 1827, Shaka's behavior grew more erratic, his cruelty extending even to his own people. During this mourning period for his mother, Shaka ordered that no crops be planted during the following year, no milk (the basis of the Zulu diet at the time) was to be drunk, and that any woman falling pregnant would be killed along with her husband.

Despite the death of Shaka in 1828, assassinated by two of his half-brothers, Zulu power continued to expand. The Anglo-Zulu War was hard-fought on January 22, 1879, and the Zulus actually defeated the British at Isandhlwana; the British, however, triumphed at Rorke's Drift later on the same day.

Text-Dependent Questions

1. Who where the Boers and what country did they originally come from?

2. Who established the Orange Free State?

of the ferocious young Zulu nation. The years 1830–34 saw the Great Trek North by the Dutch Boers in search of land to escape from British rule, the Orange Free State being established in the 1850s.

Competition for land made it difficult for Africans to move around and practice their traditional way of life, and required excess population to split off, find unclaimed land, and settle and start anew. Overstocking, excessive cropping, and drought made life impossible, and the social,

economic and political order was unable to cope with the new challenges. The Mfecane, meaning "the crushing" or "scattering," describes a period of widespread chaos and disturbance in southern Africa which, in around 1815–40, saw political changes, migrations, and wars that led not only to the emergence of the Swazi and Zulu nations, but eventually also to the founding of present-day Lesotho, Zimbabwe, Mozambique, Transvaal, and Tanzania.

The Zulu

The Zulu is a Bantu ethnic group of southern Africa. Its language is Zulu.

COLONIALISM

The French began to arrive in the Barbary states in the 1830s, and by 1848 Algeria was a *département* of France. At first, rule was modeled on the Ottoman administration, but French unemployed were encouraged to leave France in search of better prospects in North Africa. These French nationals were known as *pieds-noirs* (black-feet) and they arrived alongside Sephardic Jews and settlers from other European countries, such as Spain, Italy, and Malta, who had been born in Algeria.

Although the Muslims were officially French subjects they could not become French citizens unless they renounced Islam and converted to Christianity. Settlers, therefore, took over the land and dominated in political, economical, and educational fields.

After Algeria became independent in 1962, more than a million *pieds-noirs* returned to mainland France, where many of

BELOW: Algiers is the capital and largest city in Algeria and is situated on the Mediterranean Sea. The modern part of the city was built on level ground by the seashore. The ancient sector was constructed on a steep hill behind the modern town. The casbah or citadel is at the highest point.

OPPOSITE: Basilique Notre Dame d'Afrique, a church built by the French *Pieds-Noirs* in Algeria.

them felt ostracized, perceiving they were being blamed for causing the War of Algerian Independence and the collapse of the French Fourth Republic; similarly, they felt unable to return to Algeria because of the violence and resentment of the remaining settlers and native Algerians.

French feelings regarding colonialism were divided: the pros thought an empire would enhance French power in Europe, and the antis considered that the money and effort that would be expended

Words to understand

Bureaucracy: A system of government or business that has many complicated rules and ways of doing things.

Colonialism: The policy or practice of acquiring full or partial political control over another country, occupying it with settlers, and exploiting it economically.

Regressive: Returning to a former or less developed state.

in the process would be better spent at home.

Their defeat and the loss of Alsace-Lorraine in the Franco-Prussian War of 1870, spurred France towards gaining status, power, and colonies, causing it to pursue the *mission civilisatrice* (the civilizing mission), the notion of *rayonnement* being the spreading of French culture to enlighten others. The Maghreb was viewed as in need of such improvement, as was the rest of Africa, with the result that Tunisia was taken in 1881 and the West African colonies by 1900.

The mission was to assimilate the citizens of the colonies, turning them into model Frenchmen with no regard for their own cultures, making them abandon everything that was not French. But the French were too heavy-handed and brutal and their efforts only fostered rebellion; the majority of Africans neither became French, nor did the average Frenchman have much time for the Africans. But the fact that the African colonies sent many thousands to the aid of France during the First World War tended to create a more positive view of **colonialism**.

BELOW: The Great Mosque, Sousse, Tunisia.

OPPOSITE: Fishing boats on the Bou Regreg river and distant Casbah of the Udayas in Rabat, Morocco.

OVERLEAF: Marrakech, Morocco with the Atlas Mountains in the distance.

French rule was centralized, federal, and direct, with orders issued from Paris. The Minister for the Colonies issued orders to a Governor-General, who transmitted them to the Lieutenants-General, who in turn instructed the

administrative units, the territories run by *commandants de cercle*, who controlled officers at local level. The plan was to modernize and remake societies, enabling the people to benefit from Western science and education. It was to eradicate the African institutions the French found **regressive** and root out ignorance and superstition.

The French made less use of indigenous rulers than did the British, who adopted the status quo, finding it cheaper and more effective than installing new administrations, their experience with the Indian Civil Service proving it could run an entire sub-continent most efficiently. On the whole, the British were more relaxed than the French, planning in the long run to integrate public services, set up democratic institutions, and encourage locally owned and operated industry. There were some memorable troubles, but on the whole, the British were slower than the French to use force to stamp out opposition. In the final days of the British empire, largely peaceful transitions were achieved, with fewer bitter wars. Transition, however, was not easy in areas that had been heavily settled by Europeans, and settlers were not prepared to see countries like Kenya, Rhodesia (Zimbabwe), and South Africa go without a struggle.

The French system was cumbersome, difficult, and expensive, so expensive that Paris demanded the colonies be self-financing. Officials encouraged cash

crops and activities that would yield taxable revenue, and emigration was encouraged where a locality was not financially viable. In the final analysis, commercial interests mattered more than the grand vision. Empire must have weighed heavily on bureaucrats, for by the 1870s the French Colonial Ministry's message to Senegal was "Let us not hear from you."

It was becoming increasingly clear that many in Francophone Africa had little stomach for French rule, though some wished to retain

some cultural and economic ties. A bitter civil war finally led to Algeria becoming independent in 1962, six years after Tunisia and Morocco.

The French held on longer to their colonies than others, maintaining greater involvement after independence. This may possibly have been to maintain supplies of uranium, for 75 percent of French energy is supplied by nuclear power.

What was left behind was *La Francophonie*, 29 African countries of which 18 have French as their

An edition of *Le Petit Robert*, a French dictionary, defines colonialism as "valuing, enhancing, and exploiting the natural resources of foreign countries," which has caused some comment and attracted the ire of anti-racist groups. The British, meanwhile, cringe at the thought, being too ashamed to think about or even teach their own history sensibly.

OPPOSITE: Antananarivo is the capital of Madagascar. It was colonized by the French in 1897 until the island gained independence in 1960.

ABOVE: Gorée Island, Dakar, Senegal. The French gained control of Senegal in 1677, and like the rest of the country the island remained continuously French until 1960. The island became a base for the purchase of slaves.

The French colonized great swathes of Africa from Senegal in the west to Madagascar in the east.

official language and six where French is one of two languages, apart from which these countries having little in common. Politics, economies, and cultures may be varied, but it is deeply felt by the French that English has become an overly dominant language.

But the French still believe their role was to the good, and positive views of their colonial history are taught in schools. Of course, not all aspects of colonization were uniformly bad, and while much of it was based on a high moral purpose,

some was practical and useful: colonial governments beat off warlords and bandits, advised on land reclamation, agriculture, education, and health care, with roads, railways, bridges, and ports possibly benefiting the colonizers more than the colonized.

The British had originally been traders and have been described as "sleep-walking" into their empire. They were interested, then as now, in trade and investment, financial services, making capital investments

63

LEFT: Illustration of a convoy of ships sailing through Suez Canal. Published in L'Illustration, Journal Universel, Paris,1868.

BELOW: Shipping passing through modern the modern-day Suez Canal.

OPPOSITE: Cecil John Rhodes was a British businessman, mining magnate, and politician in South Africa, who served as prime minister of the Cape Colony from 1890 to 1896. An ardent believer in British imperialism, Rhodes and his British South Africa Company founded the southern African territory of Rhodesia (now Zimbabwe and Zambia).

OPPOSITE BELOW: Cullinan Diamond Mine in South Africa is famous for The Cullinan Diamond, mined in 1905. It is the largest, rough, gem-quality diamond ever found, at 3106.75 carats (621.350g).

abroad and developing markets. In general, the British did not see their rule as permanent, having established schools and colleges in their colonies long before they considered doing the same in Britain. This resulted in colonial cities having educated elites, who soon began challenging for power.

Although they were interested in the Suez Canal, and the gold and diamonds in South Africa, the rest of Africa was not a British priority. Nervous about the control of Suez, which was vital in their trade with India and the East, they took control of Egypt in 1882. The Union of South Africa emerged in 1910, and Cecil Rhodes dreamt of ruling from the

Cape to Alexandria, his British South Africa Company pressing north. There was a desire for a Cape–Cairo railway, which sounded like a good idea but has yet to reach completion.

In 1879–1890, the British partitioned West and East Africa. In the Scramble for Africa they eventually ended up with the largest share of empire, with nearly 30 percent of Africans coming under British control, compared with 15 percent under the French.

Today, ex-British colonies (and one former Portuguese) remain members of the Commonwealth, with many having English as a useful international lingua franca. It was Britain's intention to leave behind democratic parliaments, modeled on Westminster; a legal system; and military, police, civil and educational services based along British lines. Citizens may drive on the left and enormous numbers of them still enjoy a game of cricket.

The problem for all empire-builders was that colonies needed to be self-financing: a centralized **bureaucracy** and an army cost money and the European taxpayer was neither keen on meeting the expense, nor were African taxpayers in a position to finance such institutions; had they been forced to pay up, they might have rebelled and a rebellion was far too serious to contemplate.

Liberia: the American Colonization Society was founded in 1816 to help freed African slaves in America migrate back to Africa. Liberia was to be the "Land of the Free," but its foundation was resisted by the indigenous people of the part of West Africa where Liberia was intended to be.

The ACS closely controlled its development, but by the 1840s, Liberia had become a financial burden and the ACS was effectively bankrupt. The transported Liberians had soon become demoralized by hostile local tribes, bad management, and deadly diseases, and Liberia, moreover, was forced to consider political threats, chiefly from Britain, because it was neither a sovereign power nor the bona fide colony of any sovereign nation.

In 1847, the colony became the independent nation of Liberia in the absence of the United States declining to claim sovereignty.

The Economics of Colonialism

Economic development was a viable option, as far as colonialism was concerned, but required an assortment of approaches to fit varied administrative structures, from the light touch of indirect rule, often used by the British, to the direct rule practiced by the French in West Africa and the Belgians in the Congo; in Rhodesia there was company rule, and there was a parliamentary system with some European oversight in Egypt.

A major problem was that the world economy and the demand for commodities was changing rapidly. The car industry was now emerging, leading to a demand for rubber for tyres, while bauxite did not become useful until the inter-war period, when the use of aluminium came to the fore.

In 1901, the completion of the Uganda Railway, from the coast at Mombasa to the Lake Victoria port

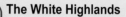

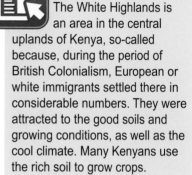

The White Highlands

The White Highlands is an area in the central uplands of Kenya, so-called because, during the period of British Colonialism, European or white immigrants settled there in considerable numbers. They were attracted to the good soils and growing conditions, as well as the cool climate. Many Kenyans use the rich soil to grow crops.

The East Africa Protectorate, founded in 1905, encouraged British immigration. By the time British Kenya was established in 1920, about 10,000 British people had colonized the area. The colony granted settlers 999-year leases over about 25 percent of the good land in Kenya.

This area was at the heart of the Mau Mau uprising, a revolt against colonial rule in Kenya, which lasted from 1952 to 1960 and helped to hasten Kenya's independence.

of Kisumu, led colonial authorities to encourage the growth of cash crops to help pay for its operating costs. Another result of the railway's construction was to transfer the eastern section of the Uganda protectorate to the Kenya colony, then called the East Africa Protectorate, to keep the entire

LEFT: Dwellings along the Mesurado River in Monrovia, Liberia.

OPPOSITE: Farmland in the Kisoro District of Uganda.

railway under one local colonial administration. Because the railway experienced cost overruns in Kenya, the British decided to justify its exceptional expense and pay its operating costs by introducing large-scale European settlement in a vast tract of land that became a center of cash-crop agriculture, known as the "White Highlands."

In much of Uganda, by contrast, agricultural production was placed in the hands of the Africans, if they responded to the opportunity. Cotton was the crop of choice, largely because of pressure from the British Cotton- Growing Association, which looked to the colonies to provide raw materials for British mills. Even the Church Missionary Society joined the effort, by launching the Uganda Company (managed by a former missionary) to promote cotton-planting and to buy and transport the produce. It was a financial success but eventually caused resentment, in that the Africans remained cotton-growers, Europeans then processed the crop, and the Indians came in as merchants, buying crops and supplying imports to the country-dwellers.

The government in East Africa was paternalistic and the people became conditioned to follow the lead offered by others. Eventually, when independence was imminent, the elite took up government service, rather than commerce, and African paternalism replaced the colonial kind.

The Invention of Africa
Africa did not offer the same kind of framework for rule as India, where the British inherited an empire, the Moghuls having been overlords in most of the continent, their rule, at times, extending into Afghanistan. As far as the British could fathom, there was an assortment of monarchs in India, and Britain made better use of existing rulers than most. The French, meanwhile, must have had a difficult time trying to incorporate republicanism into areas that once boasted their own imperial power, and *Liberté, Égalite, Fraternité* must have needed a good deal of explanation.

The British emphasized the notion of the "Great White Mother," concerned for all her imperial subjects. Queen Victoria, although interested in Africa, cared most strongly about India, the jewel in the crown, to the extent of employing a tutor to teach her Urdu, while later British monarchs were in the habit of regaling African rulers with letters and messages, rather like a father to a son.

LEFT: Cotton became the most important crop grown in the British colonies. The raw crop was used to supply the British cotton mills.

OPPOSITE: Queen Victoria as head of the British Empire was referred to as the "Great White Mother."

The British accepted that some Africans would be part of the governing class, while others would take orders and hold different positions in the hierarchy. In preparing for rule, nothing was considered more effective than public school education, a British "public" school in fact being both private and expensive. Uganda's King's College, Budo, was formed along public school lines and was (and still is) an excellent school.

Edward Mutesa (1924–69) was educated at Budo and went on to Cambridge and the army, where he was enrolled as a captain in the Grenadier Guards. He was the Kabaka of Buganda, the kabakaship being an Anglo-African institution by this time, and when he died, merited two funerals, that were conducted with full military honors both in Uganda and London.

By now, the British military had become rather more genteel than it

was in the past, and was used as a model in British Africa in the early days, later taking a back seat to the state, the professions and the business world.

The use of the military model was also prominent in French colonies, the splendidly-named Louis-Léon-César Faidherbe having been germane in establishing the French colonial empire in Africa and transforming Senegal into the dominant military and political power in West Africa. In the 1850s he had African volunteers, dressed in fetching uniforms, taking oaths on the Qur'an and listening to stories of French military triumphs; there was even the notion of providing replica uniforms for the children, to influence them in the way that they should go. Faideherbe's economic regime was able to pay for his innovations, and he was a more skilled manager than most, but others were unable to combine economic and organizational success.

But the military was not the sole focus: besides soldiers, Africans also became teachers and ministers of religion. Fourah Bay College, in Sierra Leone, was founded as early as 1827, and was a magnet for the repatriated and for Africans seeking higher education, its aims being mainly focused on the Christian ministry.

The British did not favor force to hold their empire steady, preferring the co-operation of local kings, headmen, tribal elders, and other authority figures, who would often be imbued with the almost mystical notions the British attached to their own monarchy. Honors would be given out, fêtes organized, and ceremonies, firework displays, and other jollifications were held at suitable times, these being regarded as essential in cementing members of the empire together.

Relating to and involving the people was difficult, and administrators seized on anything that could be regarded as an African tradition. Both the British and the Africans were guilty of distorting the past, which made it difficult to know what actually had existed before colonialism. It is from this invention of tradition that many came to believe that Africa had no history of its own, being a collection merely of ethnic cultures.

The ways in which Africans responded to the British were varied, although most were barely touched. Some had aspirations to be free and equal under a law which judged all equally, the latter being a novel idea in most territories in those days: important people were not judged like others.

Africans with aspirations showed loyalty to the crown and set up churches, clubs, societies, and sporting activities; others wishing to be fashionable, took up tennis or cricket. For some years, however, the notion of internationally-known black cricketers in South Africa was impossible; but there were non-white cricket teams and many Africans in the townships espoused football instead. In general, Africans excel at soccer and some West African countries regularly qualify for the World Cup.

A major incident in 1968 involved Basil D'Oliveira, a mixed-race sportsman who played cricket and football for non-white teams in South Africa. Unacceptable for inclusion in the South African national team because of his color, he moved to Britain and by 1966 had become a key member of the English team, earning his place in their team to tour South Africa in 1968–69. But the ruling body, wishing to avoid a political backlash from South Africa by naming such a player in its line-up, did not select him. This led to the international boycott of South African sport, and was a decisive factor in eventually bringing apartheid to an end. In recent years, South African cricket has revived, and is now multi-racial, while the Springboks continue to excel at international Rugby football.

Symbols of authority changed with time across pre-colonial and post-colonial eras and into present times, an example being attitudes to Shaka Zulu, who has become something of a man for all seasons. Some see him as a cruel and bloodthirsty tyrant who, through the perpetration of indescribable atrocities, gained control of other Zulu clans. Others regard him as the father of the Zulu nation, having established it in an area overdominated by whites, who at the same time showed magnanimity in permitting white traders to establish themselves at Port Natal in 1824.

The city of Johannesburg is comparable to many other cities in the West. While South Africa is a multicultural nation, European influences and the legacy of colonization are not only apparent in the structure of this city, but also in its architecture.

Text-Dependent Questions

1. What was the American Colonization Society?

2. Who were the *pied-noirs*, and where did they come from?

3. Who was the British founder of Rhodesia, (now Zimbabwe and Zambia)?

INDEPENDENCE AND NATIONHOOD

What is a nation? In general, it is a large body of people united by descent, history, culture, or language, which inhabits a particular state or territory. In pre-colonial Africa, states were created by the vagaries of the economy, while in colonial times, administrative convenience seems to have been the main criterion.

Western thought was unable to cope with the notion of subtle, stateless societies, such as those of Africa, being accustomed to nations whose charted history was of a particular people, despite the fact that such ancient kingdoms as Dahomey, Benin, that of the Ashanti in Ghana, also the kingdoms of East Africa, had once existed in Africa. **Pastoral nomads** and agriculturalists did not necessarily fit these Western notions of nationhood, so Africans were deemed to have no history of their own.

Colonial rule tended to fossilize institutions. Where kingdoms and states had risen, bloomed and

BELOW: Ashanti Yam Ceremony. A page from a book by Thomas E. Bowdich - Mission from Cape Coast Castle to Ashantee (London, 1819).

OPPOSITE ABOVE: Gezo was a King of the Kingdom of Dahomey, in present-day Benin, from 1818 until 1858.

OPPOSITE BELOW: A typical Ghanan fishing village in Axim, northern Ghana. Ghana formerly called Gold Coast was the first African country to gain independence.

Words to understand

Apartheid: (In South Africa) A policy or system of segregation or discrimination on grounds of race.

Pan-Africanism: The principle or advocacy of the political union of all the indigenous inhabitants of Africa.

Pastoral nomads: Groups who raise livestock, and they move about within their established territory to find good pastures for their animals.

rapidly waned, colonialism celebrated them, and what was regarded as "traditional" was set like a fly in amber. Africans were given tribal identities and ethnicity was restored – invented by elites and Europeans. The British believed Africans had tribes, so tribes came into being to which they could belong.

After the Second World War, colonialism in Africa was suddenly put on the defensive, when a rising tide of nationalist protest began to challenge the legitimacy of alien occupation, with the result that "development" became the more explicit goal of colonial power. Movements developed against colonialism, such as **Pan-Africanism**, while a literary movement, Négritude, came to the fore in Francophone Africa, but waned when it was seen to be promoting racial stereotyping.

The decolonization of Africa followed as colonized peoples began to agitate for independence, having come to the aid of their masters in time of war against an unknown enemy. Potential leaders came from a Western-educated elite, with men like Kenyatta in Kenya, Nkrumah in Ghana, Senghor in Senegal, and Houphouët-Boigny in the Côte d'Ivoire. Many were left-wing Marxist-Leninists and anti-imperialist pro-land reformers. Socialism was felt to be the remedy for African problems, allied against capitalism, but the spread of international capitalism and globalization was to prove unstoppable.

BELOW: Kwame Nkrumah Memorial Park in Accra, Ghana, named after Dr. Kwame Nkrumah, the founding father and first President of Ghana.

OPPOSITE ABOVE: Côte d'Ivoire President Félix Houphouët-Boigny, his wife Marie-Thérèse Houphouët-Boigny, United States First Lady Jacqueline Kennedy, and her husband US President John F. Kennedy in 1962.

OPPOSITE BELOW: Jomo Kenyatta was the leader of Kenya from its independence in 1963 to his death in 1978, serving first as prime minister (1963–64) and then as president (1964–78). He is considered the founding father of the Kenyan nation.

The first African country to gain independence was the former Gold Coast, renamed Ghana after the ancient historical empire. The first leader, from 1952, was Kwame Nkrumah, who was inspired by Gandhi and had a similar philosophy. For Nkrumah, Pan-Africanism was part of the deal: "We are going to see that we create our own African personality and identity. We again rededicate ourselves in the struggle to emancipate other countries in Africa; for our independence is meaningless unless it is linked up with the total liberation of the African continent."

But Nkrumah became far too authoritarian, as was subsequently to be the case with other leaders. In 1964 Nkrumah declared himself president for life and banned opposition parties. He was overthrown when the National

With the advent of independence in the late 1950s and early '60s, euphoria began to sweep through Africa as nation after nation attained self-determination. To most Africans this was the end of a long struggle for freedom, a dream that was soon to be shattered as government after government fell victim to coups d'état. The new military juntas accused the civilian governments of everything from corruption and incompetence to mismanagement of the national economy; but experience shows they are no better when it came to running governments, the continent having been driven into even further suffering and turmoil. They are likely to continue, as long as political and economic instability prevails.

British would have been happy to have passed it on to India. In the final days, the British couldn't dispose of their ruinously expensive empire fast enough.

To blame colonialism for the problems of Africa is to take a step too far: Ethiopia remained uncolonized and today needs more food aid than any other state, while some of the most successful parts of Africa are those that were heavily settled by Europeans, and where there was investment in infrastructure, health, education, and the promotion of some groups of people over others.

It is curious that some of the larger countries with fewer problems have never taken a lead. Some claim the artificial borders that were drawn between the states produced countries that were guaranteed to fail, and which were incapable of accepting change.

At the time of independence, there was general agreement over the need to retain borders, the problem being to create a national unity, or in Benedict Anderson's terms, an "imagined community," while others claimed that the difficulty in achieving this goal lay in ethnic, linguistic, and cultural differences.

Liberation Council (NLC) came to power in February 1966.

The international media tends to focus only on the areas of Africa where problems continue to arise, encouraging the old idea that Africans are children, who need to be instructed and who cannot be trusted to run things on their own. Some believe European wealth came from exploiting the colonies, and there is little doubt that it brought financial benefit to more than a few. The American poet and essayist, Kenneth Rexroth, shrewdly observed that the reason for the liberation of the colonies was that the colonizers had come to realize that imperialism was unprofitable. As early as 1892, the British journal, *The Economist*, had observed that "East Africa is probably an unproductive possession," and soon after the turn of the century, the

LEFT AND OPPOSITE: Desmond Tutu (left) is a South African social rights activist and retired Anglican bishop who rose to worldwide fame during the 1980s as an opponent of apartheid. He was the first to use the term "Rainbow Nation" to describe South Africa's multicultural diversity. It was later adopted by the late Nelson Mandela, South Africa's first black president pictured opposite with Nigerian journalist Kayode Soyinka.

The one country that seems to thoroughly contradict this view is South Africa – known as the "Rainbow Nation" – a term coined by Archbishop Desmond Tutu and later adopted by the then President Nelson Mandela, it being a metaphor to describe the country's newly developing multicultural diversity, following the quashing of the previous **apartheid** ideology. Today, South Africa is a nation despite its troubled past, and South Africans, whatever their background, believe this to be truly the case.

Not so very long ago, such an outcome would have seemed unimaginable, and the fact that it has happened in South Africa

Text-Dependent Questions

1. Which modern-day country was once was the ancient kingdom of the Dahomey?

2. Kwame Nkrumah was the founding father of which country?

3. Who first used the term "Rainbow Nation" to describe multicultural society in South Africa?

suggests it could happen elsewhere.

Africa has enormous manpower and resources at its disposal, if only they could be harnessed efficiently and corruption brought to an end. It would make sense, therefore, to hope that in the next 50 years, Africa will come to the fore, India and China having already shown it the way in recent years.

Index

PHOTOGRAPHIC ACKNOWLEDGEMENTS

All images in this book are supplied under license from © Shutterstock.com other than the following: Wikimedia Commons and the following contributors:- Page 10 below: Bundes Archiv, page 36 Eye Ubiquitous, page 54: JMK, page 57, page 66 David Stanley, page 75 below: Dutch National Archive, Page 76: Libris förlag, Sweden.

The content of this book was first published as *AFRICA*.

ABOUT THE AUTHOR
Annelise Hobbs

After completing her Classical studies, Annelise Hobbs became a librarian, working in a busy area of central London frequented by local authors and university students as well as the public itself. Eventually, she decided to use her extensive knowledge, and particularly her interest in travel, art, and architecture, to help in her research as an editor, inevitably progressing to writing books herself.

FIND OUT MORE:

Websites

- **Lonely Planet**
  www.lonelyplanet.com

- **Maps of Africa**
  www.worldatlas.com

- **National Geographic**
  travel.nationalgeographic.com

- **United Nations Educational, Scientific and Cultural Organization**
  http://whc.unesco.org

Further Reading by Mason Crest

AFRICA PROGRESS AND PROBLEMS
13 VOLUMES | 112 PAGES
Africa is a complex and diverse continent, and its more than 50 countries provide a study in contrasts: democracy and despotism, immense wealth and crushing poverty, modernism and traditionalism, peaceful communities and raging civil wars. The books in the AFRICA: PROGRESS AND PROBLEMS series take a close look at many of the major issues in Africa today, such as AIDS, poverty, government corruption, ethnic and religious tension, educational opportunities, and overcrowding. *2014 copyright*

THE EVOLUTION OF AFRICA'S MAJOR NATIONS
26 VOLUMES | 80 PAGES
Africa, with its rich natural resources and its incredible poverty, is a continent of contradictions. Each book in this series examines the historical and current situation of a particular African nation. Readers will learn about each country's history, geography, government, economy, cultures, and communities. *2013 copyright*